Delicious
casseroles

Delicious
casseroles

Love Food™ is an imprint of Parragon Books Ltd

Parragon
Queen Street House
4 Queen Street
Bath BA1 1HE, UK

Copyright © Parragon Books Ltd 2007

Love Food™ and the accompanying heart device is a trademark of Parragon Books Ltd

Introduction by Frances Eames
Photography by Don Last
Food Styling by Christine France

ISBN 978-1-4054-9557-8

Printed in China

Notes for the reader
• This book uses imperial, metric, and US cup measurements. Follow the same units of measurement throughout; do not mix imperial and metric.
• All spoon measurements are level: teaspoons are assumed to be 5 ml, and tablespoons are assumed to be 15 ml.
• Unless otherwise stated, milk is assumed to be lowfat and eggs are medium. The times given are an approximate guide only.
• Some recipes contain nuts. If you are allergic to nuts you should avoid using them and any products containing nuts.
• Recipes using raw or very lightly cooked eggs should be avoided by infants, the elderly, pregnant women, convalescents, and anyone suffering from illness.

Contents

Casseroles

Casseroles are the epitome of hearty, flavorsome cooking and make the perfect comfort food on a cold winter's day. Nourishing and easy to make, casseroles fit easily into a busy schedule, but produce meals that will make everyone smile.

There is a myth that slow cooking is time-consuming, but the casserole is the answer for time-pressed cooks as it can sit unattended in the oven, leaving the cook free to get on with other things.

The term casserole is derived from the French word for stew pan. The culinary term *en casserole* means "served in the vessel used for cooking" and refers to the ancient practice of stewing meat slowly in earthenware containers. Casseroles are cooked across the world from Europe to the United States, and from Africa to China.

Fuss-free
The joy of casseroles is that they are quick and easy to prepare, making them ideal for those of us with little time or inclination to prepare and cook labor-intensive meals. After a hard day at work, and the dark journey home on a winter's evening, there is nothing better than pulling a casserole from the fridge or freezer, placing it in the oven and relaxing until it's ready. And if you haven't had time to plan ahead, casseroles are still practical—just chop, fry, and stir, and the rest of the cooking is done in the oven. Preparation for casseroles has another blessing—it's the original one-pot cooking, so you won't have to clean every pan in the house after dinner.

Diverse
Casserole recipes are no longer considered budget dishes. Although they are still economical and make

good sense for feeding the family, the old idea of casseroles has faded away. The art of simple but impressive cooking to cater for family and friends is very much back on the agenda. Casserole recipes are endlessly versatile, and contrary to what you may expect, there is a huge range of possible dishes. They are also a great way to use up any leftovers in a tasty and practical way. On a cold winter's day casseroles provide a culinary hug for chilled children and hungry partners. But in summer, whenever you don't fancy yet another salad, try out some of the delicious fish and seafood recipes inside this book.

Nourishing
Casseroles are brimming with goodness, and are a great way to provide your family with healthy fare, without them noticing! Try to use vegetables that are in season to ensure you are getting the freshest ingredients, packed with vitamins. This also cuts down on your food's airmiles and your carbon footprint—you could even grow your own. It is best to use organic ingredients where possible and most supermarkets now offer organic options for most food products.

Sociable entertaining
Far from being merely weekday meals, casseroles are actually perfect for entertaining. The length of cooking time required by casserole dishes creates a blend of intense flavors that will really impress. If you have been out with friends or family for the day, you just need to spend a few minutes to assemble the dish and put it in the oven, and then you can continue to chat and relax with everyone else. Casseroles are great for feeding a hungry horde with the minimum of fuss.

Meat Casseroles

serves 4

3 tbsp olive oil

2 onions, finely sliced

2 garlic cloves, chopped

2 lb 4 oz/1 kg good-quality
braising steak

2 tbsp plain flour

10 fl oz/300 ml beef stock

bouquet garni sachet
(shop-bought)

5 fl oz/150 ml red wine

salt and pepper

1 tbsp chopped fresh parsley,
to garnish

for the herb dumplings

4 oz/115 g self-rising flour,
plus extra for shaping

2 oz/55 g suet

1 tsp mustard

1 tbsp chopped fresh parsley

1 tsp chopped fresh sage

4 tbsp cold water

stew & dumplings

Preheat the oven to 300°F/150°C. Heat 1 tablespoon of the oil in a large frying pan, add the onions and garlic and fry until softened and browned. Remove from the frying pan using a slotted spoon and place in a large casserole.

Trim the meat and cut into thick strips. Using the remaining oil, fry the meat in the frying pan over a high heat, stirring well until it is browned all over.

Sprinkle in the flour and stir well to prevent lumps. Season well with salt and pepper.

Pour in the stock, stirring constantly to make a smooth sauce, then continue to heat over a medium heat until the sauce is boiling.

Transfer the contents of the frying pan to the casserole.

Add the bouquet garni and the wine. Cover and cook in the center of the oven for 2–2$\frac{1}{2}$ hours.

Begin making the dumplings 20 minutes before the stew is ready. Place the suet and mustard in a bowl and mix well, then pour in enough of the water to form a firm but soft dough. Break the dough into 12 pieces and roll them into round dumplings (you might need some flour on your hands for this).

Remove the stew from the oven, check the seasoning, discard the bouquet garni and add the dumplings, pushing them down under the liquid. Cover and return the dish to the oven, continuing to cook for 20–25 minutes until the dumplings have doubled in size.

Serve the stew and dumplings piping hot with the parsley scattered over the top.

serves 4–6

3/4 stick butter

2 tbsp corn oil

2/3 cup smoked lardons, blanched for 30 seconds, then drained and patted dry

2 lb/900 g stewing beef, such as chuck or leg

2 large garlic cloves, crushed

1 carrot, diced

1 leek, halved and sliced

1 onion, finely chopped

2 tbsp all-purpose flour

1 1/2 cups full-bodied red Burgundy wine, such as Hermitage or Côtes du Rhône

generous 2 cups beef stock

1 tbsp tomato paste

1 fresh bouquet garni

12 pearl onions, peeled but kept whole

12 white mushrooms

salt and pepper

chopped fresh flat-leaf parsley, to garnish

beef bourguignon

Preheat the oven to 300°F/150°C. Heat 2 tablespoons of the butter and 1 tablespoon of the oil in a large, flameproof casserole. Cook the lardons over medium–high heat, stirring, for 2 minutes, or until beginning to brown. Using a slotted spoon, remove from the casserole and drain on paper towels.

Trim the beef and cut it into 2-inch/5-cm chunks. Add the beef to the casserole and cook over high heat, stirring frequently, for 5 minutes, or until browned on all sides and sealed, adding more of the butter or oil to the casserole as necessary. Using a slotted spoon, transfer the beef to a plate.

Pour off all but 2 tablespoons of the fat from the casserole. Add the garlic, carrot, leek, and chopped onion and cook over medium heat, stirring frequently, for 3 minutes, or until the onion is beginning to soften. Sprinkle in the flour, and salt and pepper to taste, and cook, stirring constantly, for 2 minutes, then remove the casserole from the heat.

Gradually stir in the wine and stock and add the tomato paste and bouquet garni, then return to the heat and bring to a boil, stirring and scraping any sediment from the bottom of the casserole.

Return the beef and lardons to the casserole and add extra stock if necessary so that the ingredients are covered by about 1/2 inch/1 cm of liquid. Slowly return to a boil, then cover and cook in the preheated oven for 2 hours.

Meanwhile, heat 2 tablespoons of the remaining butter and the remaining oil in a large sauté pan or skillet and cook the pearl onions over medium–high heat, stirring frequently, until golden all over. Using a slotted spoon, transfer the onions to a plate.

Heat the remaining butter in the pan and cook the mushrooms, with salt and pepper to taste, stirring frequently, until golden brown. Remove from the pan and then stir them, with the onions, into the casserole. Re-cover and cook for an additional 30 minutes, or until the beef is very tender. Serve garnished with parsley,.

serves 6

2 tbsp olive oil

1 lb/450 g pearl onions, peeled but kept whole

2 garlic cloves, halved

2 lb/900 g stewing beef, cubed

1/2 tsp ground cinnamon

1 tsp ground cloves

1 tsp ground cumin

2 tbsp tomato paste

generous 3 cups full-bodied red wine

grated rind and juice of 1 orange

1 bay leaf

salt and pepper

1 tbsp chopped fresh flat-leaf parsley, to garnish

boiled or mashed potatoes, to serve

beef & pearl onion casserole

Preheat the oven to 300°F/150°C. Heat the oil in a large, flameproof casserole and cook the whole onions and garlic, stirring frequently, for 5 minutes, or until softened and beginning to brown. Add the beef and cook over high heat, stirring frequently, for 5 minutes, or until browned on all sides and sealed.

Stir the spices and tomato paste into the casserole and add salt and pepper to taste. Pour in the wine, scraping any sediment from the bottom of the casserole, then add the orange rind and juice and the bay leaf. Bring to a boil and cover.

Cook in the preheated oven for about 1 1/4 hours. Remove the lid and cook the casserole for an additional hour, stirring once or twice, until the meat is tender. Remove from the oven and garnish with the parsley. Serve hot, accompanied by boiled or mashed potatoes.

serves 4

1 lb/450 g lean boneless
lamb, such as leg of lamb
or fillet

1½ tbsp all-purpose flour

1 tsp ground cloves

1–1½ tbsp olive oil

1 white onion, sliced

2–3 garlic cloves, sliced

1¼ cups orange juice

⅔ cup lamb stock or
chicken stock

1 cinnamon stick, bruised

2 sweet (pointed, if available)
red bell peppers, seeded and
sliced into rings

4 tomatoes

salt and pepper

few fresh sprigs cilantro, plus
1 tbsp chopped fresh
cilantro, to garnish

lamb stew with sweet red peppers

Preheat the oven to 375°F/190°C. Trim any fat or gristle from the lamb and cut into thin strips. Mix the flour and cloves together. Toss the lamb in the spiced flour until well coated and reserve any remaining spiced flour.

Heat 1 tablespoon of the oil in a heavy-bottom skillet and cook the lamb over high heat, stirring frequently, for 3 minutes, or until browned on all sides and sealed. Using a slotted spoon, transfer to an ovenproof casserole.

Add the onion and garlic to the skillet and cook over medium heat, stirring frequently, for 3 minutes, adding the extra oil if necessary. Sprinkle in the reserved spiced flour and cook, stirring constantly, for 2 minutes, then remove from the heat. Gradually stir in the orange juice and stock, then return to the heat and bring to a boil, stirring.

Pour over the lamb in the casserole, then add the cinnamon stick, red bell peppers, tomatoes, and cilantro sprigs and stir well. Cover and cook in the preheated oven for 1½ hours, or until the lamb is tender.

Discard the cinnamon stick and adjust the seasoning to taste. Serve garnished with the chopped cilantro.

serves 4

pinch of saffron threads

2 tbsp almost boiling water

1 lb/450 g lean boneless
lamb, such as leg steaks

1 1/2 tbsp all-purpose flour

1 tsp ground coriander

1/2 tsp ground cumin

1/2 tsp ground allspice

1 tbsp olive oil

1 onion, chopped

2–3 garlic cloves, chopped

scant 2 cups lamb or
chicken stock

1 cinnamon stick, bruised

1/2 cup dried apricots,
coarsely chopped

6 oz/175 g zucchini, sliced
into half moons

4 oz/115 g cherry tomatoes

1 tbsp chopped fresh cilantro

salt and pepper

2 tbsp coarsely chopped
pistachios, to garnish

couscous, to serve

mediterranean lamb with apricots & pistachios

Put the saffron threads in a heatproof pitcher with the water and let stand for at least 10 minutes to infuse. Trim off any fat or gristle from the lamb and cut into 1-inch/2.5-cm chunks. Mix the flour and spices together, then toss the lamb in the spiced flour until well coated and reserve any remaining spiced flour.

Heat the oil in a large, heavy-bottom pan and cook the onion and garlic, stirring frequently, for 5 minutes, or until softened.

Add the lamb and cook over high heat, stirring frequently, for 3 minutes, or until browned on all sides and sealed. Sprinkle in the reserved spiced flour and cook, stirring constantly, for 2 minutes, then remove from the heat.

Gradually stir in the stock and the saffron and its soaking liquid, then return to the heat and bring to a boil, stirring. Add the cinnamon stick and apricots. Reduce the heat, then cover and simmer, stirring occasionally, for 1 hour.

Add the zucchini and tomatoes and cook for an additional 15 minutes. Discard the cinnamon stick. Stir in the fresh cilantro and season to taste with salt and pepper. Serve sprinkled with the pistachios, accompanied by couscous.

serves 4

4 lamb shanks, about
12 oz/350 g each

6 garlic cloves

2 tbsp extra-virgin olive oil

1 tbsp fresh rosemary,
very finely chopped

salt and pepper

4 red onions

12 oz/350 g carrots, cut into
thin sticks

4 tbsp water

lamb shanks with roasted onions

Preheat the oven to 350°F/180°C. Trim off any excess fat from the lamb shanks. Using a small, sharp knife, make 6 cuts in each. Cut the garlic cloves lengthwise into 4 slices. Insert 6 garlic slices into the cuts in each lamb shank.

Put the lamb in a single layer in a roasting pan, drizzle with the oil, sprinkle with the rosemary, and season to taste with pepper. Roast in the preheated oven for 45 minutes.

Wrap each of the onions in a piece of foil. Remove the roasting pan from the oven and season the lamb to taste with salt. Return to the oven and put the wrapped onions on the shelf next to it. Roast for an additional 1–1¼ hours until the lamb is very tender.

Meanwhile, bring a large pan of water to a boil. Add the carrot sticks and blanch for 1 minute. Drain and refresh in cold water.

Remove the roasting pan from the oven when the lamb is meltingly tender and transfer to a warmed serving dish. Skim off any fat from the roasting pan and put the pan over medium heat. Add the carrots and cook, stirring, for 2 minutes, then add the water and bring to a boil. Reduce the heat and simmer, stirring constantly and scraping any sediment from the bottom of the pan.

Transfer the carrots and sauce to the serving dish. Remove the onions from the oven and unwrap. Cut off and discard about ½ inch/1 cm of the tops and add the onions to the serving dish. Serve immediately.

serves 4

12 oz/350 g lean pork fillet

1 tbsp vegetable oil

1 medium onion, chopped

2 garlic cloves, crushed

2 tbsp all-purpose flour

2 tbsp tomato paste

generous 1¾ cups chicken or vegetable stock

4½ oz/125 g white mushrooms, sliced

1 large green bell pepper, seeded

½ tsp freshly grated nutmeg, plus extra to garnish

4 tbsp lowfat plain yogurt

salt and pepper

boiled rice with chopped fresh parsley, to serve

pork stroganoff

Trim away any excess fat and silver skin from the pork, then cut the meat into ½-inch/1-cm thick slices. Heat the vegetable oil in a large, heavy-bottom skillet and gently cook the pork, onion, and garlic for 4–5 minutes, or until lightly browned.

Stir in the flour and tomato paste, then pour in the chicken stock and stir to mix thoroughly. Add the mushrooms, bell pepper, salt and pepper to taste, and nutmeg. Bring to a boil, cover, and let simmer for 20 minutes, or until the pork is tender and cooked through.

Remove the skillet from the heat and stir in the yogurt. Transfer the pork to 4 large, warmed serving plates and serve with boiled rice sprinkled with chopped fresh parsley and an extra spoonful of yogurt, garnished with freshly grated nutmeg.

serves 4

1 lb/450 g lean boneless pork

1¹/₂ tbsp all-purpose flour

1 tsp ground coriander

1 tsp ground cumin

1¹/₂ tsp ground cinnamon

1 tbsp olive oil

1 onion, chopped

14 oz/400 g canned chopped tomatoes

2 tbsp tomato paste

2 cups chicken stock

8 oz/225 g carrots, chopped

12 oz/350 g squash, such as kabocha, peeled, seeded, and chopped

8 oz/225 g leeks, sliced, blanched, and drained

4 oz/115 g okra, trimmed and sliced

salt and pepper

sprigs of fresh parsley, to garnish

couscous, to serve

pork & vegetable stew

Trim off any fat or gristle from the pork and cut into thin strips about 2 inches/5 cm long. Mix the flour and spices together. Toss the pork in the spiced flour until well coated and reserve any remaining spiced flour.

Heat the oil in a large, heavy-bottom pan and cook the onion, stirring frequently, for 5 minutes, or until softened. Add the pork and cook over high heat, stirring frequently, for 5 minutes, or until browned on all sides and sealed. Sprinkle in the reserved spiced flour and cook, stirring constantly, for 2 minutes, then remove from the heat.

Gradually add the tomatoes to the pan. Blend the tomato paste with a little of the stock in a pitcher and gradually stir into the pan, then stir in half the remaining stock.

Add the carrots, then return to the heat and bring to a boil, stirring. Reduce the heat, then cover and simmer, stirring occasionally, for 1¹/₂ hours. Add the squash and cook for an additional 15 minutes.

Add the leeks and okra, and the remaining stock if you prefer a thinner stew. Simmer for an additional 15 minutes, or until the pork and vegetables are tender. Season to taste with salt and pepper, then garnish with fresh parsley and serve with couscous.

serves 4

1–1 lb 4 oz/450–550 g lean gammon

1–2 tbsp olive oil, plus 1–2 tsp

1 onion, chopped

2–3 garlic cloves, chopped

2 celery stalks, chopped

6 oz/175 g sliced carrots

1 cinnamon stick, bruised

1/2 tsp ground cloves

1/4 tsp freshly grated nutmeg

1 tsp dried oregano

pepper

scant 2 cups chicken stock or vegetable stock

1–2 tbsp maple syrup

3 large, spicy sausages, about 8 oz/225 g, or chorizo (outer casing removed)

14 oz/400 g canned black-eye peas or fava beans

1 orange bell pepper

1 tbsp cornstarch

ham with black-eye peas

Trim off any fat or skin from the ham and cut into 1$\frac{1}{2}$-inch/ 4-cm chunks. Heat 1 tablespoon oil in a heavy-bottom pan and cook the ham over high heat, stirring frequently, for 5 minutes, or until browned on all sides and sealed. Using a slotted spoon, remove from the pan and set aside.

Add the onion, garlic, celery, and carrots to the pan with an additional 1 tablespoon oil if necessary and cook over medium heat, stirring frequently, for 5 minutes, or until softened. Add all the spices and season with pepper to taste, then cook, stirring constantly, for 2 minutes.

Return the ham to the pan. Add the dried oregano, stock, and maple syrup to taste, then bring to a boil, stirring. Reduce the heat, then cover and simmer, stirring occasionally, for 1 hour.

Heat the remaining 1–2 teaspoons oil in a skillet and cook the sausages, turning frequently, until browned all over. Remove and cut each into 3–4 chunks, then add to the pan. Drain and rinse the peas, then drain again. Seed and chop the orange bell pepper. Add the beans and bell pepper to the pan, and simmer for an additional 20 minutes. Blend 2 tablespoons of water with the cornstarch and stir into the stew, then cook for 3–5 minutes. Discard the cinnamon stick and serve.

serves 6

scant 5/8 cup all-purpose
flour

3 lb/1.3 kg pork tenderloin,
cut into 1/4-inch/5-mm slices

4 tbsp sunflower-seed oil

2 onions, thinly sliced

2 garlic cloves, finely
chopped

14 oz/400 g canned chopped
tomatoes in juice

1 1/2 cups dry white wine

1 tbsp torn fresh basil leaves

2 tbsp chopped fresh parsley,
plus extra sprigs to garnish

salt and pepper

fresh crusty bread, to serve

pork casserole

Spread the flour out on a plate and season to taste with salt and
pepper. Toss the pork slices in the flour to coat, shaking off any
excess. Heat the oil in an ovenproof casserole over medium heat.
Add the pork slices and cook until browned all over. Using a
slotted spoon, transfer the pork to a plate.

Add the onions to the casserole and cook over low heat, stirring
occasionally, for 10 minutes, or until golden brown. Add the
garlic and cook, stirring, for 2 minutes, then add the tomatoes
with their juice, the wine, and basil leaves, and season to taste
with salt and pepper. Cook, stirring frequently, for 3 minutes.

Return the pork to the casserole, cover, and simmer gently for
1 hour, or until the meat is tender. Stir in the chopped parsley.
Serve immediately, garnished with parsley sprigs, and accompanied
by fresh crusty bread.

2

Poultry & Game Casseroles

serves 4

2 tbsp butter

8 pearl onions

4 1/2 oz/125 g lean bacon, coarsely chopped

4 fresh chicken joints

1 garlic clove, finely chopped

12 white mushrooms

1 1/4 cups red wine

1 bouquet garni

1 tbsp chopped fresh tarragon

salt and pepper

2 tsp cornstarch

chopped fresh flat-leaf parsley, to garnish

coq au vin

Melt half of the butter in a large skillet over medium heat. Add the onions and bacon and cook, stirring, for 3 minutes. Lift out the bacon and onions and set aside. Melt the remaining butter in the pan and add the chicken. Cook for 3 minutes, then turn over and cook on the other side for 2 minutes.

Drain off any excess chicken fat. Return the bacon and onions to the pan, then add the garlic, mushrooms, red wine, and herbs. Season with salt and pepper. Cook for about 1 hour, or until cooked through. Remove from the heat, lift out the chicken, onions, bacon, and mushrooms, transfer them to a serving platter, and keep warm. Discard the bouquet garni.

Mix the cornstarch with 1–2 tablespoons of water, then stir it into the juices in the pan. Bring to a boil, lower the heat, and cook, stirring, for 1 minute. Pour the sauce over the chicken and serve, garnished with parsley.

serves 4

1¹/₂ tbsp unsalted butter

2 tbsp olive oil

4 lb skinned chicken portions, bone in

2 red onions, sliced

2 garlic cloves, chopped finely

14 oz canned tomatoes, chopped

2 tbsp chopped fresh flat-leaf parsley

6 fresh basil leaves, torn

1 tbsp sun-dried tomato paste

²/₃ cup red wine

salt and pepper

8 oz mushrooms, sliced

chicken, tomato & onion casserole

Melt the butter with the olive oil in a flameproof casserole dish. Add the chicken pieces and cook, turning frequently, for 5–10 minutes, until golden brown all over. Transfer the pieces to a plate, using a slotted spoon.

Add the onions and garlic to the casserole and cook over low heat, stirring occasionally, for 10 minutes, until golden. Add the tomatoes with the juice from the can, the parsley, basil leaves, tomato paste, and wine, and season to taste with salt and pepper. Bring to a boil, then return the chicken pieces to the casserole, pushing them down into the sauce.

Cover and cook in a preheated oven, 325°F/160°C, for 50 minutes. Add the mushrooms and cook for an additional 10 minutes, until the chicken is cooked through and tender. Serve immediately.

serves 4

4 chicken portions, about
5¹/2 oz/150 g each, skinned if
preferred

1 tbsp olive oil

1 onion, chopped

2 celery stalks, coarsely
chopped

1¹/2 tbsp all-purpose flour

1¹/4 cups clear apple juice

²/3 cup chicken stock

1 baking apple, cored and
cut into quarters

2 bay leaves

1–2 tsp clear honey

1 yellow bell pepper, seeded
and cut into chunks

1 tbsp butter

1 large or 2 medium eating
apples, cored and sliced

2 tbsp raw brown sugar

salt and pepper

1 tbsp chopped fresh mint,
to garnish

chicken & apple pot

Preheat the oven to 375°F/190°C. Lightly rinse the chicken and pat dry with paper towels.

Heat the oil in a deep skillet and cook the chicken over medium–high heat, turning frequently, for 10 minutes, or until golden all over and sealed. Using a slotted spoon, transfer to an ovenproof casserole.

Add the onion and celery to the skillet and cook over medium heat, stirring frequently, for 5 minutes, or until softened. Sprinkle in the flour and cook, stirring constantly, for 2 minutes, then remove from the heat.

Gradually stir in the apple juice and stock, then return to the heat and bring to a boil, stirring. Add the cooking apple, bay leaves, and honey and season to taste.

Pour over the chicken in the casserole, then cover and cook in the preheated oven for 25 minutes. Add the bell pepper and cook for an additional 10–15 minutes, or until the chicken is tender and the juices run clear when a skewer is inserted into the thickest part of the meat.

Meanwhile, preheat the broiler to high. Melt the butter in a pan over low heat. Line the broiler pan with kitchen foil. Brush the eating apple slices with half the butter, then sprinkle with a little sugar and cook under the broiler for 2–3 minutes, or until the sugar has caramelized. Turn the slices over. Brush with the remaining butter and sprinkle with the remaining sugar, and cook for an additional 2 minutes. Serve the stew garnished with the apple slices and mint.

serves 4

4 tbsp sunflower oil

2 lb/900 g chicken meat, chopped

3 cups white mushrooms, sliced

16 shallots

6 garlic cloves, chopped finely

1 tbsp all-purpose flour

1 cup white wine

1 cup chicken bouillon

1 fresh bouquet garni, with sage and 1 celery stalk

14 oz/400 g canned borlotti beans, drained and rinsed

salt and pepper

steamed squash, to serve

garlic chicken casserole

Heat the sunflower oil in an ovenproof casserole and sauté the chicken until browned all over. Remove the chicken from the casserole with a draining spoon and set aside until required.

Add the mushrooms, shallots, and garlic to the casserole and cook for 4 minutes.

Return the chicken to the casserole and sprinkle with the flour, then cook for another 2 minutes.

Add the white wine and chicken bouillon, stir until boiling, then add the bouquet garni. Season with salt and pepper to taste.

Add the beans to the casserole.

Cover and place in the center of a preheated oven, 300°F/150°C, for 2 hours. Remove the bouquet garni and serve the casserole with the squash.

serves 4

3 tbsp olive oil

5 lb/2.5 kg chicken, cut into 8 pieces and dusted with flour

7 oz/200 g fresh chorizo sausages, thickly sliced

a small bunch of fresh sage leaves

1 onion, chopped

6 garlic cloves, sliced

2 celery stalks, sliced

1 small pumpkin or butternut squash, peeled and roughly chopped

1 cup dry sherry

2½ cups chicken stock

14 oz/400 g canned chopped tomatoes

2 bay leaves

salt and pepper

a small bunch of fresh flat-leaf parsley, chopped

chicken, pumpkin & chorizo casserole

Preheat the oven to 350°F/180°C.

Heat the oil in a casserole dish and fry the chicken with the chorizo and sage leaves, until golden brown. Remove with a slotted spoon and reserve. You may need to do this in two batches.

Add the onion, garlic, celery, and pumpkin and cook until the mixture begins to brown slightly.

Add the sherry, chicken stock, tomatoes, and bay leaves, and season with salt and pepper to taste.

Return the reserved chicken, chorizo, and sage to the casserole, cover, and cook in the oven for 1 hour.

Remove the casserole from the oven, uncover, stir in the chopped parsley and serve.

serves 4

4 whole chicken legs, dusted in flour

1 tbsp olive oil

1 tbsp butter

1 onion, chopped

3 garlic cloves, sliced

4 parsnips, peeled and cut into large chunks

1 cup dry white wine

3½ cups chicken stock

3 leeks, white parts only, sliced

3 oz/85 g prunes, halved (optional)

1 tbsp English mustard

1 bouquet garni

salt and pepper

3½ oz/100 g fresh bread crumbs

3 oz/85 g feta cheese, crumbled

2 oz/55 g mixed chopped tarragon and flat-leaf parsley

chicken casserole with a herb crust

Preheat oven to 350°F/180°C.

Fry the chicken in a casserole dish with the olive oil and butter, until golden brown. Remove with a slotted spoon and keep warm.

Add the onion, garlic, and parsnips to the casserole and cook until slightly browned.

Add the wine, stock, leeks, prunes, if using, mustard, and bouquet garni, and season with salt and pepper to taste.

Return the chicken to the casserole, cover, and cook in the oven for 1 hour.

Mix the breadcrumbs, cheese, and herbs together.

Remove the casserole from the oven and increase the oven temperature to 400°F/200°C.

Sprinkle the casserole with the bread crumb mixture and return to the oven for 10 minutes, uncovered, until the crust starts to brown slightly.

Remove from the oven and serve.

duckling with lentils

serves 4

1 duckling, weighing 5 lb/2.25 kg

generous 1 1/8 cups brown lentils

1 tbsp virgin olive oil

2 onions

2 celery stalks

2 tbsp brandy or grappa

2/3 cup dry white wine

1 tsp cornstarch

salt and pepper

for the stock

wings, backbone, and neck from the duckling

1 celery stalk

1 garlic clove

large pinch of salt

6 peppercorns, lightly crushed

1 bay leaf

5 fresh flat-leaf parsley sprigs

1 onion

1 clove

Cut the duckling into joints. Cut off the wings. Fold back the skin at the neck end and cut out the wishbone with a small, sharp knife. Using poultry shears or heavy kitchen scissors, cut the breast in half along the breastbone, from the tail end to the neck. Cut along each side of the backbone to separate the 2 halves. Remove the backbone. Cut each portion in half diagonally.

To make the stock, put the wings, backbone, and neck, if available, in a large pan and add the celery, garlic, peppercorns, bay leaf, and parsley. Stick the onion with the clove and add to the pan with the salt. Add cold water to cover and bring to a boil. Skim off any scum that rises to the surface, then reduce the heat and simmer very gently for 2 hours. Strain into a clean pan and boil until reduced and concentrated. Set aside the stock, keeping 2/3 cup separate from the rest.

Rinse the lentils and place in a pan. Add cold water to cover and the oil. Halve an onion and add with a celery stalk. Bring to a boil, then reduce the heat and simmer for 15 minutes, or until the lentils are beginning to soften. Drain and set aside.

Meanwhile, put the duckling pieces, skin-side down, in a heavy-bottom skillet and cook, gently shaking the skillet occasionally, for 10 minutes. Transfer to an ovenproof casserole and drain off the excess fat from the skillet. Finely chop the remaining onion and celery and add to the skillet. Cook over a low heat, stirring occasionally, for 5 minutes, or until softened. Using a slotted spoon, transfer the vegetables to the casserole.

Set the casserole over medium heat, add the brandy, and ignite. When the flames have died down, add the wine and the reserved measured stock. Bring to a boil, add the lentils, and season to taste with pepper. Cover and simmer gently over low heat for 40 minutes, until the lentils and duck are tender and the juices run clear when a skewer is inserted into the thickest part of the meat.

Blend the cornstarch with 2 tablespoons of the remaining reserved stock to a smooth paste in a small bowl. Stir the paste into the casserole and cook, stirring constantly, for 5 minutes, or until thickened. Add the salt to taste and adjust the seasoning, if necessary. Serve immediately.

serves 4

4 duck portions, about
5¹/₂ oz/150 g each

1–2 tsp olive oil, plus
1 tbsp (optional)

1 red onion, cut into wedges

2–3 garlic cloves, chopped

1 large carrot, chopped

2 celery stalks, chopped

2 tbsp all-purpose flour

1¹/₄ cups red wine, such as
claret

2 tbsp brandy (optional)

²/₃–generous ³/₄ cup stock or
water

salt and pepper

3-inch/7.5-cm strip of orange
rind

2 tsp redcurrant jelly

4 oz/115 g sugarsnap peas

4 oz/115 g white mushrooms

1 tbsp chopped fresh parsley,
to garnish

duck & red wine stew

Remove and discard the fat from the duck. Lightly rinse and pat dry with paper towels.

Heat a large, deep skillet for 1 minute until warm but not piping hot. Put the duck portions in the skillet and heat gently until the fat starts to run. Increase the heat a little, then cook, turning over halfway through, for 5 minutes, or until browned on both sides and sealed. Using a slotted spoon, transfer the duck portions to a flameproof casserole.

Add 1 tablespoon of the oil if there is little duck fat in the skillet and cook the onion, garlic, carrot, and celery, stirring frequently, for 5 minutes, or until softened. Sprinkle in the flour and cook, stirring constantly, for 2 minutes, then remove the skillet from the heat.

Gradually stir in the wine, brandy (if using), and stock, then return to the heat and bring to a boil, stirring. Season to taste with salt and pepper, then add the orange rind and redcurrant jelly. Pour over the duck portions in the casserole, then cover and simmer, stirring occasionally, for 1–1¹/₄ hours.

Cook the sugarsnap peas in a pan of boiling water for 3 minutes, then drain and add to the stew. Meanwhile, heat 1–2 teaspoons of the olive oil in a small pan and cook the mushrooms, stirring frequently, for 3 minutes, or until beginning to soften. Add to the stew. Cook the stew for an additional 5 minutes, or until the duck is tender. Serve garnished with the parsley.

serves 4

4 duck breasts, about
5 1/2 oz/150 g each

2 tbsp olive oil

8 oz/225 g piece ham, cut
into small chunks

8 oz/225 g chorizo, outer
casing removed

1 onion, chopped

3 garlic cloves, chopped

3 celery stalks, chopped

1–2 fresh red chiles, seeded
and chopped

1 green bell pepper, seeded
and chopped

2 1/2 cups chicken stock

1 tbsp chopped fresh oregano

14 oz/400 g canned chopped
tomatoes

1–2 tsp hot pepper sauce,
or to taste

fresh sprigs of parsley,
to garnish

green salad and freshly
cooked long-grain rice,
to serve

duck jambalaya-style stew

Remove and discard the skin and any fat from the duck breasts.
Cut the flesh into bite-size pieces.

Heat half the oil in a large deep skillet and cook the duck, ham,
and chorizo over high heat, stirring frequently, for 5 minutes,
or until browned on all sides and sealed. Using a slotted spoon,
remove from the skillet and set aside.

Add the onion, garlic, celery, and chiles to the skillet and cook
over medium heat, stirring frequently, for 5 minutes, or until
softened. Add the green bell pepper, then stir in the stock,
oregano, tomatoes, and hot pepper sauce.

Bring to a boil, then reduce the heat and return the duck,
ham, and chorizo to the skillet. Cover and simmer, stirring
occasionally, for 20 minutes, or until the duck and ham
are tender.

Drain and serve with the Jambalaya, garnished with parsley and
accompanied by a green salad and rice.

serves 6

3 tbsp olive oil

2 lb 4 oz/1 kg casserole venison, cut into 1¹/₄-inch/ 3-cm cubes

2 onions, peeled and thinly sliced

2 garlic cloves, peeled and chopped

1¹/₂ cups beef or vegetable stock

2 tbsp all-purpose flour

¹/₂ cup port or red wine

2 tbsp red currant jelly

6 juniper berries, crushed

4 cloves, crushed

pinch of cinnamon

small grating of nutmeg

salt and pepper

chopped parsley, to garnish

baked or mashed potatoes, to serve

venison casserole

Preheat the oven to 350°F/180°C. Heat the oil in a large skillet and cook the cubes of venison over high heat for 2–3 minutes until brown. You may need to cook the meat in two or three batches— do not overcrowd the skillet. Remove the venison from the skillet using a slotted spoon and place in the casserole dish.

Add the onion and garlic to the skillet and cook over medium heat for about 3 minutes until a good golden color, then lift out, and add to the meat.

Gradually add the stock to the skillet, stir well, and scrape up the sediment, then bring to a boil.

Sprinkle the meat in the casserole dish with the flour and turn to coat evenly.

Add the hot stock to the casserole and stir well, making sure that the meat is just covered.

Add the wine, red currant jelly, and the spices.

Season well, cover, and cook gently in the center of the preheated oven for 2–2¹/₂ hours.

Remove from the oven, check the seasoning, and adjust if necessary. Garnished with chopped parsley and serve immediately with baked or mashed potatoes.

3

Fish & Seafood Casseroles

serves 4

1 yellow bell pepper, 1 red bell pepper, 1 orange bell pepper, seeded and cut into quarters

1 lb/450 g ripe tomatoes

2 large, fresh, mild green chiles, such as poblano

6 garlic cloves, peeled but kept whole

2 tsp dried oregano or dried mixed herbs

2 tbsp olive oil, plus extra for drizzling

1 large onion, finely chopped

scant 2 cups fish stock, vegetable or chicken stock

finely grated rind and juice of 1 lime

2 tbsp chopped fresh cilantro, plus extra to garnish

1 bay leaf

1 lb/450 g red snapper fillets, skinned and cut into chunks

8 oz/225 g raw shrimp, shelled and deveined

8 oz/225 g raw squid rings

salt and pepper

warmed flour tortillas, to serve

south-western seafood stew

Preheat the oven to 400°F/200°C. Put the pepper quarters, skin-side up, in a roasting pan with the tomatoes, chiles, and garlic. Sprinkle with the oregano and drizzle with oil. Roast in the preheated oven for 30 minutes, or until the bell peppers are well browned and softened.

Remove the roasted vegetables from the oven and let stand until cool enough to handle. Peel off the skins from the bell peppers, tomatoes, and chiles and chop the flesh. Finely chop the garlic.

Heat the oil in a large pan and cook the onion, stirring frequently, for 5 minutes, or until softened. Add the bell peppers, tomatoes, chiles, garlic, stock, lime rind and juice, cilantro, bay leaf, and salt and pepper to taste. Bring to a boil, then stir in the fish and seafood. Reduce the heat, then cover and simmer gently for 10 minutes, or until the fish and squid are just cooked through and the shrimp have turned pink. Discard the bay leaf, then garnish with chopped cilantro before serving, accompanied by warmed flour tortillas.

serves 4

2 tbsp olive oil

1 large onion, finely chopped

pinch of saffron threads

$1/2$ tsp ground cinnamon

1 tsp ground coriander

$1/2$ tsp ground cumin

$1/2$ tsp ground turmeric

7 oz/200 g canned chopped
tomatoes

$1^1/4$ cups fish stock

4 small red snappers,
cleaned, boned, and heads
and tails removed

2 oz/55 g pitted green olives

1 tbsp chopped preserved
lemon

3 tbsp chopped fresh cilantro

salt and pepper

moroccan fish tagine

Heat the olive oil in a flameproof casserole. Add the onion
and cook gently over very low heat, stirring occasionally, for
10 minutes, or until softened, but not colored. Add the saffron,
cinnamon, ground coriander, cumin, and turmeric and cook
for an additional 30 seconds, stirring constantly.

Add the tomatoes and fish stock and stir well. Bring to a boil,
reduce the heat, cover, and simmer for 15 minutes. Uncover and
simmer for 20–35 minutes, or until thickened.

Cut each red snapper in half, then add the fish pieces to the
casserole, pushing them down into the liquid. Simmer the stew
for an additional 5–6 minutes, or until the fish is just cooked.

Carefully stir in the olives, lemon, and fresh cilantro. Season to
taste with salt and pepper and serve immediately.

serves 8

2 lb 12 oz/1.25 kg sea bass, filleted, skinned, and cut into bite-size chunks

2 lb 12 oz/1.25 kg redfish, filleted, skinned, and cut into bite-size chunks

3 tbsp extra-virgin olive oil

grated rind of 1 orange

1 garlic clove, finely chopped

pinch of saffron threads

2 tbsp pastis, such as Pernod

1 lb/450 g live mussels

1 large cooked crab

1 small fennel bulb, finely chopped

2 celery stalks, finely chopped

1 onion, finely chopped

5 cups fish stock

8 oz/225 g small new potatoes, scrubbed

8 oz/225 g tomatoes, peeled, seeded, and chopped

1 lb/450 g large raw shrimp, shelled and deveined

salt and pepper

bouillabaisse

Put the fish pieces in a large bowl and add 2 tablespoons of the oil, the orange rind, garlic, saffron, and pastis. Toss the fish pieces until well coated, then cover and let marinate in the refrigerator for 30 minutes.

Meanwhile, clean the mussels by scrubbing or scraping the shells and pulling out any beards that are attached to them. Discard any with broken shells or any that refuse to close when tapped. Remove the meat from the crab, then chop and reserve.

Heat the remaining oil in a large, flameproof casserole and cook the fennel, celery, and onion over low heat, stirring occasionally, for 5 minutes, or until softened. Add the stock and bring to a boil. Add the potatoes and tomatoes and cook over medium heat for 7 minutes.

Reduce the heat and add the fish to the stew, beginning with the thickest pieces, then add the mussels, shrimp, and crab and simmer until the fish is opaque, the mussels have opened, and the shrimp have turned pink. Discard any mussels that remain closed. Season to taste with salt and pepper and serve immediately.

serves 6

2 tbsp sunflower-seed or corn oil

6 oz/175 g okra, trimmed and cut into 1-inch/2.5-cm pieces

2 onions, finely chopped

4 celery stalks, very finely chopped

1 garlic clove, finely chopped

2 tbsp all-purpose flour

1/2 tsp sugar

1 tsp ground cumin

salt and pepper

3 cups fish stock

1 red bell pepper and 1 green bell pepper, seeded and chopped

2 large tomatoes, chopped

12 oz/350 g large raw shrimp

4 tbsp chopped fresh parsley

1 tbsp chopped fresh cilantro

dash of Tabasco sauce

12 oz/350 g cod or haddock fillets, skinned

12 oz/350 g monkfish fillet

louisiana gumbo

Heat half the oil in a large, flameproof casserole, or large pan with tightly fitting lid, and cook the okra over low heat, stirring frequently, for 5 minutes, or until browned. Using a slotted spoon, remove the okra from the casserole and set aside.

Heat the remaining oil in the casserole and cook the onion and celery over medium heat, stirring frequently, for 5 minutes, or until softened. Add the garlic and cook, stirring, for 1 minute. Sprinkle in the flour, sugar, and cumin and add salt and pepper to taste. Cook, stirring constantly, for 2 minutes, then remove from the heat.

Gradually stir in the stock and bring to a boil, stirring. Return the okra to the casserole and add the bell peppers and tomatoes. Partially cover, then reduce the heat to very low and simmer gently, stirring occasionally, for 10 minutes. Meanwhile, shell and devein the shrimp and reserve.

Add the herbs and Tabasco sauce to taste. Cut the cod and monkfish into 1-inch/2.5-cm chunks, then gently stir into the stew. Stir in the shrimp. Cover and simmer gently for 5 minutes, or until the fish is cooked through and the shrimp have turned pink. Transfer to a large, warmed serving dish and serve.

serves 4–6

7 oz/200 g dried ribbon egg pasta, such as tagliatelle

2 tbsp butter

1 cup fine fresh bread crumbs

14 fl oz/400 ml canned condensed cream of mushroom soup

1/2 cup milk

2 celery stalks, chopped

1 red bell pepper, seeded and chopped

1 green bell pepper, seeded and chopped

1 1/4 cups coarsely grated sharp Cheddar cheese

2 tbsp chopped fresh parsley

7 oz/200 g canned tuna in oil, drained and flaked

salt and pepper

tuna & noodle casserole

Preheat the oven to 400°F/200°C. Bring a large pan of salted water to a boil. Add the pasta, then return to a boil and cook for 2 minutes less than specified on the package directions.

Meanwhile, melt the butter in a separate small pan. Stir in the bread crumbs, then remove from the heat and set aside.

Drain the pasta well and set aside. Pour the soup into the pasta pan over medium heat, then stir in the milk, celery, bell peppers, half the cheese, and all the parsley. Add the tuna and gently stir in so that the flakes don't break up. Season to taste with salt and pepper. Heat just until small bubbles appear around the edge of the mixture—do not boil.

Stir the pasta into the pan and use 2 forks to mix all the ingredients together. Spoon the mixture into an ovenproof dish that is also suitable for serving and spread it out.

Stir the remaining cheese into the buttered bread crumbs, then sprinkle over the top of the pasta mixture. Bake in the preheated oven for 20–25 minutes, or until the topping is golden. Remove from the oven, then let stand for 5 minutes before serving straight from the dish.

serves 6

2 tbsp olive oil

1 red onion, peeled and sliced

2 garlic cloves, peeled and chopped

2 red bell peppers

14 oz/400 g canned chopped tomatoes

1 tsp chopped fresh oregano or marjoram

a few saffron threads soaked in 1 tbsp warm water for 2 minutes

1 lb/450 g white fish (cod, haddock, or hake), skinned and boned

1 lb/450 g prepared squid, cut into rings

1¼ cups fish or vegetable stock

1 cup cooked shelled shrimp

salt and pepper

chunky bread, to serve

6 cooked whole shrimp in their shells and 2 tbsp chopped fresh parsley, to garnish

mediterranean fish casserole

Heat the oil in a skillet and cook the onion and garlic over medium heat for 2–3 minutes until beginning to soften.

Seed and thinly slice the bell peppers and add to the skillet. Continue to cook over low heat for 5 minutes more. Add the tomatoes with the herbs and saffron and stir well.

Preheat the oven to 400°F/200°C. Cut the white fish into 1¼-inch/3-cm pieces and place with the squid in the casserole dish. Pour in the cooked vegetable mixture and the stock, stir well, and season to taste.

Cover and cook in the center of the preheated oven for about 30 minutes until the fish is tender and cooked. Add the shrimp at the last minute and just heat through.

Serve in hot bowls garnished with the whole shrimp and the parsley. Provide lots of chunky bread to mop up the casserole juices.

serves 4

4 tbsp lemon juice

6 tbsp olive oil

salt and pepper

4 swordfish steaks, about
6 oz/175 g each

1 onion, finely chopped

1 garlic clove, finely chopped

1 tbsp all-purpose flour

8 oz/225 g tomatoes, peeled,
seeded, and chopped

1 tbsp tomato paste

1¼ cups dry white wine

fresh dill sprigs, to garnish

spanish fish in tomato sauce

Preheat the oven to 350°F/180°C. Place the lemon juice and 4 tablespoons of the olive oil in a shallow, nonmetallic dish, stir well, then season to taste with salt and pepper. Add the swordfish steaks, turning to coat thoroughly, then cover with plastic wrap and let marinate in the refrigerator for 1 hour.

Heat the remaining oil in a flameproof casserole. Add the onion and cook over low heat, stirring occasionally, for 10 minutes, or until golden. Add the garlic and cook, stirring frequently, for 2 minutes. Sprinkle in the flour and cook, stirring, for 1 minute, then add the tomatoes, tomato paste, and wine. Bring to a boil, stirring.

Add the fish to the casserole, pushing it down into the liquid. Cover and cook in the preheated oven for 20 minutes, or until cooked through and the flesh flakes easily. Serve garnished with dill sprigs.

serves 4

3¹/₂ tbsp butter, plus extra for greasing

5 tbsp all-purpose flour

1 tsp mustard powder

2¹/₂ cups milk

2 tbsp olive oil

1 onion, chopped

2 garlic cloves, finely chopped

1 lb/450 g mixed mushrooms, sliced

²/₃ cup white wine

14 oz/400 g canned chopped tomatoes

salt and pepper

1 lb/450 g skinless white fish fillets

8 oz/225 g ready-prepared fresh scallops

4–6 sheets fresh lasagna

8 oz/225 g mozzarella cheese, chopped

seafood lasagna

Preheat the oven to 400°F/200°C. Melt the butter in a pan over low heat. Add the flour and mustard powder and stir until smooth. Simmer gently for 2 minutes without coloring. Gradually add the milk, whisking until smooth. Bring to a boil, reduce the heat, and simmer for 2 minutes. Remove from the heat and reserve. Cover the surface of the sauce with plastic wrap to prevent a skin forming.

Heat the oil in a skillet. Add the onion and garlic and cook gently for 5 minutes, or until softened. Add the mushrooms and cook for 5 minutes, or until softened. Stir in the wine and boil rapidly until almost evaporated, then stir in the tomatoes. Bring to a boil, reduce the heat, and simmer, covered, for 15 minutes. Season and reserve.

Cut the fish into cubes. Grease a lasagna dish, spoon half the tomato mixture over the bottom, top with half the fish and scallops, and layer half the lasagna over the top. Pour over half the white sauce and sprinkle over half the mozzarella. Repeat these layers, finishing with sauce and mozzarella.

Bake in the preheated oven for 35–40 minutes, or until golden and the fish is cooked through. Remove from the oven and let stand for 10 minutes before serving.

serves 6

1 lb/450 g live mussels

6 squid

1/2 cup olive oil

1 Spanish onion, chopped

2 garlic cloves, finely chopped

1 red bell pepper, seeded and cut into strips

1 green bell pepper, seeded and cut into strips

14 oz/400 g risotto rice

2 tomatoes, peeled and chopped

1 tbsp tomato paste

6 oz/175 g monkfish fillet, cut into chunks

6 oz/175 g red snapper fillet, cut into chunks

6 oz/175 g cod fillet, cut into chunks

generous 2 cups fish stock

4 oz/115 g fresh or frozen green beans, halved

4 oz/115 g fresh or frozen peas

6 canned artichoke hearts, drained

1/4 tsp saffron threads

salt and pepper

12 raw jumbo shrimp

paella del mar

Clean the mussels by scrubbing or scraping the shells and pulling off any beards. Discard any with broken shells or any that refuse to close when tapped with a knife. Rinse the mussels under cold running water.

To prepare each squid, pull the pouch and tentacles apart, then remove the innards from the pouch. Slice the tentacles away from the head and discard the head. Rinse the pouch and tentacles under cold running water and slice.

Heat the oil in a paella pan or flameproof casserole. Add the onion, garlic, and bell peppers. Cook over medium heat, stirring, for 5 minutes, or until softened. Add the squid and cook for 2 minutes. Add the rice and cook, stirring, until transparent and coated with oil.

Add the tomatoes, tomato paste, and fish and cook for 3 minutes, then add the stock. Gently stir in the beans, peas, artichoke hearts, and saffron and season to taste with salt and pepper.

Arrange the mussels around the edge of the pan and top the mixture with the shrimp. Bring to a boil, reduce the heat, and simmer, shaking the pan from time to time, for 15–20 minutes, or until the rice is tender. Discard any mussels that remain closed and serve.

makes 4–6

1 onion, chopped

2 celery stalks, sliced

3 garlic cloves, sliced

4 tbsp olive oil

1 tbsp smoked paprika

1 small pinch of saffron strands

1 cup dry sherry

2 1/2 cups chicken or fish stock

2 bay leaves

14 oz/400 g canned chopped tomatoes

1 lb 8 oz/500 g waxy potatoes, peeled and cut into quarters

salt and pepper

2 red bell peppers, seeded and sliced

3 lb/1.5 kg mixed seafood of your choice (whole shrimp, squid, mussels, monkfish, and salmon)

1 lemon, finely grated, and some chopped fresh flat-leaf parsley, for sprinkling

extra-virgin olive oil, for drizzling

rustic fish stew

Gently sweat the onions, celery, and garlic with the olive oil in a medium-size saucepan with a lid, until translucent (about 10 minutes).

Add the smoked paprika and saffron strands and cook for an additional minute, then add the sherry and reduce by half.

Add the stock, bay leaves, tomatoes, and potatoes. Season with salt and pepper to taste and cook for 10 minutes, or until the potatoes are almost cooked.

Add the peppers and cook for an additional 10 minutes.

Carefully add the seafood, stirring only once or twice. Place the lid on the pan and cook for 8–10 minutes, or until the seafood is cooked through.

Remove from the heat and let stand for a few moments.

Serve the stew in a large bowl, sprinkled with the lemon and parsley. Season with pepper to taste and drizzle with olive oil.

4

Vegetable Casseroles

serves 8

1 red cabbage, about
1 lb 10 oz/750 g

2 onions, peeled and thinly
sliced

1 garlic clove, peeled and
chopped

2 small cooking apples,
peeled, cored, and sliced

2 tbsp molasses sugar

1/2 tsp ground cinnamon

whole nutmeg, for grating

2 tbsp red wine vinegar

rind and juice of 1 orange

salt and pepper

2 tbsp red currant jelly

red cabbage casserole

Preheat the oven to 300°F/150°C. Cut the cabbage into quarters and remove the center stalk. Shred the leaves finely.

In the casserole dish, layer the red cabbage, onions, garlic, and apples. Sprinkle with the sugar and cinnamon and grate a quarter of the nutmeg over the top.

Pour in the wine vinegar and orange juice and sprinkle the orange rind on top.

Stir well and season. The dish will be quite full, but the volume of the cabbage will reduce during cooking.

Cook in the center of the preheated oven for 1–1 1/2 hours, stirring from time to time. If you prefer, you can cook it more quickly in a flameproof casserole dish on the stovetop over medium heat for 8–10 minutes until the cabbage is just tender. The stove method leaves the cabbage crunchier.

Stir in the red currant jelly, and adjust the seasoning if necessary. Serve hot.

serves 4

1 eggplant, cut into 1-inch/2.5-cm slices

1 tbsp olive oil, plus extra for brushing

1 large red or yellow onion, finely chopped

2 red or yellow bell peppers, seeded and finely chopped

3–4 garlic cloves, finely chopped or crushed

1 lb 12 oz/800 g canned chopped tomatoes

1 tbsp mild chili powder

1/2 tsp ground cumin

1/2 tsp dried oregano

salt and pepper

2 small zucchini, cut into fourths lengthwise and sliced

14 oz/400 g canned kidney beans, drained and rinsed

scant 2 cups water

1 tbsp tomato paste

6 scallions, finely chopped

scant 1 1/4 cups grated Cheddar cheese

vegetable chili

Brush the eggplant slices on one side with oil. Heat half the oil in a large, heavy-bottom skillet. Add the eggplant slices, oiled-side up, and cook over medium heat for 5–6 minutes, or until browned on one side. Turn the slices over, cook on the other side until browned, and transfer to a plate. Cut into bite-size pieces.

Heat the remaining oil in a large pan over medium heat. Add the chopped onion and bell peppers to the pan and cook, stirring occasionally, for 3–4 minutes, or until the onion is just softened, but not browned. Add the garlic and cook for an additional 2–3 minutes, or until the onion just begins to color.

Add the tomatoes, chili powder, cumin, and oregano. Season to taste with salt and pepper. Bring just to a boil, reduce the heat, cover, and simmer gently for 15 minutes.

Add the zucchini, eggplant, and kidney beans. Stir in the water and tomato paste. Return to a boil, then cover the pan and simmer for an additional 45 minutes, or until the vegetables are tender. Taste and adjust the seasoning, if necessary.

Ladle into warmed bowls and top with chopped scallions and cheese.

serves 4

¹/4 cup butter

2 leeks, sliced

2 carrots, sliced

2 potatoes, cut into bite-size pieces

1 rutabaga, cut into bite-size pieces

2 zucchini, sliced

1 fennel bulb, halved and sliced

2 tbsp all-purpose flour

15 oz canned lima beans

2¹/2 cups vegetable stock

2 tbsp tomato paste

1 tsp dried thyme

2 bay leaves

salt and pepper

for the dumplings

generous ³/4 cup self-rising flour

pinch of salt

¹/2 cup vegetarian suet

2 tbsp chopped fresh parsley

about 4 tbsp water

cold weather vegetable casserole

Melt the butter in a large, heavy-bottom pan over a low heat. Add the leeks, carrots, potatoes, rutabaga, zucchini, and fennel and cook, stirring occasionally, for 10 minutes. Stir in the flour and cook, stirring constantly, for 1 minute. Stir in the can juice from the beans, the stock, tomato paste, thyme, and bay leaves and season to taste with salt and pepper. Bring to a boil, stirring constantly, then cover and simmer for 10 minutes.

Meanwhile, make the dumplings. Sift the flour and salt into a bowl. Stir in the suet and parsley, then add enough water to bind to a soft dough. Divide the dough into 8 pieces and roll into balls. Add the lima beans and dumplings to the pan, cover, and simmer for a further 30 minutes. Remove and discard the bay leaves before serving.

serves 4

4 garlic cloves

1 small acorn squash

1 red onion, sliced

2 leeks, sliced

1 eggplant, sliced

1 small celery root, diced

2 turnips, sliced

2 plum tomatoes, chopped

1 carrot, sliced

1 zucchini, sliced

2 red bell peppers

1 fennel bulb, sliced

6 oz/175 g Swiss chard

2 bay leaves

1/2 tsp fennel seeds

1/2 tsp chili powder

pinch each of dried thyme, dried oregano, and sugar

1/2 cup extra-virgin olive oil

scant 1 cup vegetable stock

1 oz/25 g fresh basil leaves, torn

4 tbsp chopped fresh parsley

salt and pepper

2 tbsp freshly grated Parmesan cheese, to serve

Italian vegetable stew

Finely chop the garlic and dice the squash. Put them in a large, heavy-bottom pan with a tight-fitting lid. Add the onion, leeks, eggplant, celery root, turnips, tomatoes, carrot, zucchini, red bell peppers, fennel, Swiss chard, bay leaves, fennel seeds, chili powder, thyme, oregano, sugar, oil, stock, and half the basil to the pan. Mix together well, then bring to a boil.

Reduce the heat, then cover and simmer for 30 minutes, or until all the vegetables are tender.

Sprinkle in the remaining basil and the parsley and season to taste with salt and pepper. Serve immediately, sprinkled with the cheese.

serves 4

6 Chinese dried mushrooms

9¹/2 oz/275 g bean curd

3 tbsp vegetable oil

1 carrot, cut into thin strips

1¹/2 cups snow peas

10–12 baby corn ears, halved lengthwise

8 oz/225 g canned sliced bamboo shoots, drained

1 red bell pepper, cut into chunks

1 cup Napa cabbage, shredded

1 tbsp soy sauce

1 tbsp black bean sauce

1 tsp sugar

salt and pepper

1 tsp cornstarch

vegetable oil for deep-frying

9 oz/250 g Chinese rice noodles

black bean casserole

Soak the dried mushrooms in a bowl of warm water for 20–25 minutes. Drain and squeeze out the excess water, reserving the liquid. Remove the tough centers and slice the mushrooms thinly.

Cut the bean curd into cubes, then boil in a pan of lightly salted water for 2–3 minutes to firm up, and drain.

Heat half the vegetable oil in a pan. Add the bean curd and cook until lightly browned. Remove and drain on paper towels.

Add the remaining vegetable oil and stir-fry the mushrooms, carrot, snow peas, baby corn, bamboo shoots, and bell pepper for 2–3 minutes. Add the Napa cabbage and bean curd, and continue to stir-fry for a further 2 minutes.

Stir in the soy and black bean sauces and the sugar, and season with a little salt. Add 6 tbsp of the reserved mushroom liquid mixed with the cornstarch. Bring to a boil, reduce the heat, cover, and braise for about 2–3 minutes, until the sauce thickens slightly.

Heat the oil for deep-frying in a large pan. Deep-fry the noodles, in batches, until puffed up and lightly golden. Drain and serve with the casserole.

serves 6

generous 1 cup dried navy beans, soaked overnight and drained

6 tbsp olive oil

2 large onions, sliced

2 garlic cloves, chopped

2 bay leaves

1 tsp dried oregano

1 tsp dried thyme

5 tbsp red wine

2 tbsp tomato paste

3½ cups vegetable bouillon

8 oz/225 g dried penne, or other short pasta shapes

2 celery stalks, sliced

1 fennel bulb, sliced

scant 2 cups sliced mushrooms

8 oz/225 g tomatoes, sliced

salt and pepper

1 tsp dark molasses sugar

scant 1 cup dry white bread crumbs

salad greens and crusty bread, to serve

pasta & bean casserole

Place the beans in a pan, cover with water, and bring to a boil. Boil rapidly for 20 minutes, then drain.

Place the beans in a large flameproof casserole, stir in 5 tablespoons of the olive oil, the onions, garlic, bay leaves, herbs, wine, and tomato paste, and pour in the vegetable bouillon.

Bring to a boil, then cover the casserole, and bake in a preheated oven, 350°F/180°C, for 2 hours.

Towards the end of the cooking time, bring a large pan of salted water to the boil, add the pasta and the remaining olive oil and cook for 3 minutes. Drain and set aside.

Remove the casserole from the oven and add the pasta, celery, fennel, mushrooms, and tomatoes, and season to taste with salt and pepper.

Stir in the sugar and sprinkle over the bread crumbs. Cover the casserole, return to the oven, and continue cooking for 1 hour. Serve hot with salad greens and crusty bread.

serves 4

8 oz/225 g dried cannellini
beans

2 tbsp olive oil

4–8 baby onions, halved

2 celery stalks, cut into
1/4-inch/5-mm slices

8 oz/225 g baby carrots,
scrubbed and halved if large

10 1/2 oz/300 g new potatoes,
scrubbed and halved, or cut
into quarters if large

3 3/4–5 cups vegetable stock

1 fresh bouquet garni

1 1/2–2 tbsp light soy sauce

3 oz/85 g baby corn

1 cup frozen or shelled fresh
fava beans, thawed if frozen

salt and pepper

1/2–1 savoy or spring (Primo)
cabbage, about 8 oz/225 g

1 1/2 tbsp cornstarch

2 tbsp cold water

2–3 oz/55–85 g Parmesan
or sharp Cheddar cheese,
grated, to serve

spring stew

Pick over the cannellini beans and rinse thoroughly, then drain and put in a large bowl. Cover with plenty of cold water and let soak overnight. The next day, drain, put in a pan and cover with cold water. Bring to a boil and boil rapidly for 10 minutes, then drain and set aside.

Heat the oil in a large, heavy-bottom pan with a tight-fitting lid, and cook the vegetables, stirring frequently, for 5 minutes, or until softened. Add the stock, drained beans, bouquet garni, and soy sauce, then bring to a boil. Reduce the heat, then cover and simmer for 12 minutes.

Add the baby corn and fava beans and season to taste with salt and pepper. Simmer for an additional 3 minutes.

Meanwhile, discard the outer leaves and hard central core from the cabbage and shred the leaves. Add to the pan and simmer for an additional 3–5 minutes, or until all the vegetables are tender.

Blend the cornstarch with the water, then stir into the pan and cook, stirring, for 4–6 minutes, or until the liquid has thickened. Serve the cheese separately, for stirring into the stew.

serves 4

10 cloves

1 onion, peeled but kept whole

1$\frac{1}{8}$ cups Puy or green lentils

1 bay leaf

6$\frac{1}{4}$ cups vegetable stock

2 leeks, sliced

2 potatoes, diced

2 carrots, chopped

3 zucchini, sliced

1 celery stalk, chopped

1 red bell pepper, seeded and chopped

salt and pepper

1 tbsp lemon juice

vegetable & lentil casserole

Preheat the oven to 350°F/180°C. Press the cloves into the onion. Put the lentils into a large casserole, then add the onion and bay leaf and pour in the stock. Cover and cook in the preheated oven for 1 hour.

Remove the onion and discard the cloves. Slice the onion and return it to the casserole with the vegetables. Stir thoroughly and season to taste with salt and pepper. Cover and return to the oven for 1 hour.

Discard the bay leaf. Stir in the lemon juice and serve straight from the casserole.

serves 4

1 tbsp olive oil, for brushing

1 lb 8 oz potatoes

2 leeks

2 beefsteak tomatoes

8 fresh basil leaves

1 garlic clove, finely chopped

salt and pepper

1¼ cups vegetable stock

layered vegetable casserole

Preheat the oven to 350°F/180°C. Brush a large flameproof dish with a little of the olive oil. Prepare all the vegetables. Peel and thinly slice the potatoes, trim and thinly slice the leeks, and slice the tomatoes.

Place a layer of potato slices in the bottom of the dish, sprinkle with half of the basil leaves and cover with a layer of leeks. Top with a layer of tomato slices. Repeat these layers until all the vegetables are used up, ending with a layer of potatoes. Stir the chopped garlic into the vegetable stock and season to taste with salt and pepper. Pour the stock over the vegetables and brush the top with the remaining olive oil.

Bake in the preheated oven for 1½ hours, or until the vegetables are tender and the topping is golden brown. Serve immediately.

serves 4

¹/4 cup sun-dried tomatoes, chopped

1¹/8 cups Puy lentils

2¹/2 cups cold water

2 tbsp olive oil

¹/2–1 tsp crushed dried chiles

2–3 garlic cloves, chopped

1 large onion, cut into small wedges

1 small celery root, cut into small chunks

8 oz/225 g carrots, sliced

8 oz/225 g new potatoes, scrubbed and cut into chunks

1 small acorn squash, seeded, peeled, and cut into small chunks, about 8 oz/ 225 g prepared weight

2 tbsp tomato paste

1¹/4 cups vegetable stock

1–2 tsp hot paprika

few fresh sprigs of thyme

1 lb/450 g ripe tomatoes

sour cream and crusty bread, to serve

vegetable goulash

Put the sun-dried tomatoes in a small heatproof bowl, then cover with almost boiling water and let soak for 15–20 minutes. Drain, reserving the soaking liquid. Meanwhile, rinse and drain the lentils, then put them in a pan with the cold water and bring to a boil. Reduce the heat, then cover and simmer for 15 minutes. Drain and set aside.

Heat the oil in a large, heavy-bottom pan, with a tight-fitting lid, and cook the chiles, garlic, and vegetables, stirring frequently, for 5–8 minutes, or until softened. Blend the tomato paste with a little of the stock in a pitcher and pour over the vegetable mixture, then add the remaining stock, lentils, the sun-dried tomatoes and their soaking liquid, and the paprika and thyme.

Bring to a boil, then reduce the heat and simmer, covered, for 15 minutes. Add the fresh tomatoes and simmer for an additional 15 minutes, or until the vegetables and lentils are tender. Serve topped with spoonfuls of sour cream, accompanied by crusty bread.